June has been recognized as one of the top real estate Brokers all 50 years of her career. Read on for just a few of the many reviews she has received:

June inspires great admiration
from all who come in contact with her. We love her!

Betsey and Arty S, Connecticut

June is the all-time best real estate broker!

Marty and Jeffrey C, Florida

Knowledge, integrity, passion, energy, honesty, generosity, humor, flair... June's recipes for a long and successful real estate career.

Ann S, Maine

I continue to be amazed at the incredible energy and intelligence June brings to every decision.

Patricia E, Florida

June is one of a kind!

Bill W, Florida

Here's to June Rosenthal, the turquoise lady, on an amazing 50 year career. You are a tremendous inspiration to us all.

Rob V, Maryland

June is unquestionably the best there is! She is poised, classy, kind, smart and aggressive.

Amy and Howard F, Connecticut

June was the best and most helpful broker ever!

Daryl and David C., Florida

Thank you for your professionalism and follow up all these years.

Judy and David K, Massachusetts

Here is the ultimate real estate broker who always responded to the demands and desires of her clients.

Jay S, Connecticut

She is the consummate real estate agent and a treasured friend.

Rayna and Jack H, Connecticut

We will be forever grateful for June's integrity.

Degan and Dave S, Florida

Watching June do her homework, listen and learn about the people on all sides of the transaction, and having everyone trust and respect her is watching a true artist at work.

Rick R, Connecticut

June Rosenthal is truly a remarkable person in every imaginable way.

Tom R, Connecticut

I treasure her acumen. Whether buying selling or renting, she manages these transactions with wisdom and integrity. Her patience and kindness truly go "above and beyond."

Gwen K, Connecticut

In my experience in Connecticut, there was nobody better than June.

Harry D, Connecticut

As a mentor, June guided this builder through many real estate transactions.

John D, Connecticut

HOUSE$ FOR LOVE & MONEY

Stories & Lessons from a Remarkable
50-year Career in Real Estate

JUNE ROSENTHAL

DEDICATION

A HUGE thank you to my two gifted children... Jan and Reid... for their continuing faith in my being able to accomplish new feats in my 90s.

Reid, the true author in our family, has inspired me to create a book to match his best seller - *Land for Love and Money*

Hence...my *Houses for Love and Money!* A good duo for researching and delivering extraordinary information that will tickle your heart and fatten your wallet... A fun read!

Truly a mother/son double bonanza!

PREFACE

At age 96 and being a 50-year residential broker with more than 2,000 transactions under my belt, I've enjoyed numerous real estate experiences which I will now share with you. The world of real estate is as complex as are the human beings who buy and sell houses. Dealing with so many distinctive personalities is indeed challenging. However, finding the right home for the buyer or helping a seller find the right buyer is the result of hands-on hard work. Quiet power is what makes it all happen. In other words, being aggressive in a gentle, calm, assertive way rather than being blunt, pushy and combative.

Real estate is never monotonous or boring. Every single transaction is a novel experience. Buyers' and sellers' wants and needs are totally distinctive…engaged mortgage brokers and attorneys are completely different personalities as well – and dealing with each and every one of these people can be daunting. However, the end result of helping the seller or buyer to attain their goal is unbelievably rewarding – and the commission check is the gift for making it all happen.

To me, being a successful residential real estate broker is being able to set the buyer or seller at ease so they are more relaxed and trusting. Educating them about the marketplace and gaining their confidence is even more important. Just imagine when it is both YOUR listing and YOUR buyer - that's when trust is the most important ingredient in your work ethic.

Being a "people person" was always easy for me, but maintaining a professional demeanor at the same time was much more difficult. The incredible array of good friends I have made throughout the years is most fulfilling of all. I am still in touch with so many people from 20-30-40 years ago... as evidenced by my amazing holiday card list of 350. Just imagine, I presently live 2,200 miles away from my old home and real estate career. I do have a wonderful partner still there, who has boots on the ground, and we both belong to this fine firm who bought the real estate business I created. BUT I find it remarkable that I am all that distance away, 96 years young, and I still attract business!

I have included TEACHING STORIES in this book. They are tagged and are at the beginning of the story-telling episodes. Hopefully they will contribute to a much easier learning process for you than it was for me!

TABLE OF CONTENTS

—◆—

June Rosenthal

PART I

PREPARING TO ENTER THE FIELD

Real Estate: *A Profession or a Hobby?*

—————

A Teaching Story

If you are entering the residential real estate field as a hobby—making a little spending money, enjoy seeing houses, meeting people, having flexible hours of employment, working only when you feel like it—then this teaching vignette is not for you. For those of you who want to be professionals, this is a must read.

The real estate business is complex with unexpected nuances. To be an excellent agent/broker is sometimes overwhelming. You must know the inventory, be able to work with different personalities (buyers, sellers, other agents, attorneys, bank/mortgage personnel, inspectors), and know real estate's rules and regulations— and do the written work of creating tantalizing listings, buyers' and sellers' agreements, inspections, and a whole host of other computer-prompted papers. These tasks take enormous time away from contacting people to list and sell.

If you are sincerely trying to be an outstanding agent, earning the money that comes with that title, then the answer is to hire a good assistant. They will be able to do all the very time-consuming written work and relieve you of other necessary every day duties which would take your time away from what you do best: listing and selling. That frees you up for meeting your clients' needs: making contacts, attending open houses to assess the market properly, and the business of marketing and branding yourself so that you stand out. All of this takes time, patience and smart thinking. One does not just "go into" the real estate world. Plan it out and give it much thought as you take your introductory courses to obtain your professional license. It is a superlative vocation for the right personality, but definitely not for everyone.

If you think you can regulate your hours from 9-5, 5 days a week, then the residential real estate business is not for you. This is the world where the customer/client *always* comes first...which day, which hour is their prerogative—and you must be ready to accommodate their wishes. Many times, it means 7 days a week—sometimes early mornings or evening showings and occasionally even holidays. The point is, you are on call, much like doctors used to be. And if you don't put yourself out there, there are many other agents who can and will take your place. You truly need to be focused on "accommodation." This quality is extremely impressive to buyers and sellers alike. They will remember you as someone dedicated to helping them achieve their real estate goals. That is the ultimate reward and compliment.

To sum it up, an assistant is truly helpful. Be prepared to work hard and be at the beck and call of your customers/clients. You will be remembered for your knowledge and dedication to the business. And if you treat all your people with respect and humility, they are likely to stay with you forever.

Owning Your Own Office
or
Being a Realtor in Someone Else's Office

A Teaching Story

Sometimes, there is a strong desire to be the broker/president of your very own real estate company. I had that calling, but it took 15 years of working for another agency before I was really ready.

There are all sorts of things to consider before becoming a real estate CEO. Will you also list and sell, along with your agents—or will they find fault with that idea? They may think you should be giving them all of those leads you are getting. How much will they have to pay the company for ads and other marketing? What kind of commission split will they be given? (of course they always want bigger.) They will come to you for questions and advice—and you need to know the answers. All of this knowledge comes with the valuable experience of working with others and learning everything you can.

Working as a Realtor in an agency in the beginning is not only wise, but it truly may be the best way to continue your real estate career. Having no worries of owning your own business and con-centrating on listings and sales is probably the wisest use of your time, certainly in the beginning of your career. You will have plenty of time to decide what is best for you. You might be sur-prised at how your views can change radically as you launch your-self into the real estate world.

A Beginning With No End

A Teaching Story

Real Estate is truly the most remarkable business. The diversity itself keeps the whole process exciting. One day you can have a young, newly-engaged couple just beginning life together, and the next day you have a married couple planning a renovation to accommodate a new member of the family or a middle-aged couple deciding to purchase a more elaborate home for their family or change their lifestyle for more comfort—and finally the older couple whose children are creating their own livelihoods and these parents have decided on downsizing or retirement and a whole new way of life.

From young to old, you have the unique responsibility of contributing to satisfaction at each stage of peoples' lives. It is an important and empowering task, but it's a quiet power that lies underneath the surface. Having within you the patience, empathy and knowledge will allow you to handle each of these stages with poise and confidence. Your clients will appreciate being in your care as you work hard to satisfy their needs.

Keeping in touch with your clients from the early years on is so vitally important. Once you have established that close relationship, you are pledged to help them forever...from answering questions to physically helping with solutions, you are the "go to" person for answers. There is no money involved - just sincere help and advice. You have earned their trust and friendship and will become a fixture in their real estate life - perhaps even become true friends outside of real estate. But you must be genuine; otherwise they will see through you and view your actions as just another business ploy. However, your authentic engagement with them post-sale is very rewarding, as you undoubtedly reap benefits equal to, or perhaps more than what they receive from you. That's the rewarding part...those giving years undoubtedly benefit you more than it does them!

This generates a strong, uplifting feeling of knowing that you are trusted and respected and gives never-ending joy and fulfillment to the real estate field! For the past 6 years I have lived 2,200 miles away from my real estate contacts - at my age of 96 – yet I still attract my former buyers/sellers for their real estate needs. In my mind, that proves the validity of this teaching.

People, Homes and History

People are what make our real estate world so precious. Upon moving to another neighborhood, we became friends with our neighbors. 25 years before that I had made arrangements with a lovely lady to watch our son when our daughter was being born. I found out years later that this new neighbor's mother was the wonderful lady who stayed with our son. They lived on a corner where the road is named for their family. Much earlier she lived on a large family farm on that road. Her Great Uncle Harold, who also lived on that farm, explored the South Pole with Admiral Richard E. Byrd, the famous explorer. A peak in Antarctica bears Harold's name, June Nunatak...so much history with this one wonderful family.

Real Estate is so fascinating and intriguing...I have been involved with all of this family's real estate needs —listing, selling, renting for so many years. This special family is the soul of my 60 year community. Every day, she and her dear husband do a good deed for someone else. It's their mantra for living life well. We developed a friendship over the years that will be forever ours. Many times we would get together for soup, salad and dessert—and loved every minute of our togetherness.

There are so many special people in this world that you are lucky enough to meet and enjoy for a lifetime. God Bless Real Estate!

Marketplace Trends

A Teaching Story

Keeping up with the news and paying careful attention to glitches in various marketplaces is a good way to be aware of change—both sudden and future.

Occasionally, my husband and I had a Saturday night indoor round robin doubles tennis event….so much fun. One planned evening, we were tired and really sorry we had signed up. Well, we went and was that ever a lucky evening for me!

After playing with one partner, it was time for snacks and rest. We all sat around eating and gabbing when my last partner singled me out and asked if I knew of any good investment condominiums available because he would like to buy a few. That was 1983. We met that Monday, and he bought his first two! In less than a month, he bought twenty more. I became known as "The Condo Kid." All from one Saturday evening tennis group!

That should have been the ultimate in lucky timing, but there's more…In the first few months of 1987, my customer called me to put every one of those 22 condos on the market. I was stunned, but listed them all—a few at a time. Within six months, we sold them all, so he made a hefty profit before the housing crash of late 1987 and beginning of 1988! How did he know? I can only guess he was astute at market trends and had it figured out. I learned from that scenario and began paying much more attention to signs in the marketplace. Keeping up with news and trends makes you a better real estate agent.

For example: your good client calls you in September to let you know he will be listing his home the following May and he needs your help to get his home ready for sale. Ordinarily, that would be perfect timing, giving the broker and seller plenty of time to get ready.

However, if through your updates and constant vigil of real estate trends, you felt uneasy about next summer's marketplace, you might talk with your seller in person about your uncertainty. You might encourage him to go on the market sooner—perhaps immediately if sales were happening when he called, or maybe listing much earlier in the next year, instead of waiting until May. Many times, that type of diligence is a lifesaver for your trusting client. It takes courage and conviction to put yourself out on a swaying branch, but your customers/clients never forget. Their trust in you is forever…there is no greater reward in your real estate career.

Famous Architect

Several good builders in my area were my clients. One in particular chose me as listing broker for 12 houses in a luxury subdivision. A famous architect was chosen for these high-end homes. The builder, the bank partners, the lawyers and excited "me" all went into the big city to meet with the architect at his office.

He kept us waiting quite a while and then appeared like a king in his court. I had made a list of important features that sold well in our area. He was very rude to me and said he knew what people were looking for and his houses satisfied all buyers. My group knew me well and were very annoyed that he spoke to me that way. I told them not to worry…I was fine and didn't take it personally.

Well, the first home went up, and we had a huge open house to show it off. Of course, the architect was there. I had told the builder that the biggest flaw I saw was the second floor maid's room with a stairway from the kitchen which had no connection to the second floor children's bedrooms. The builder agreed and mentioned this to the architect, who blew up at the thought that anyone would find fault with his layout! He never did change it. A few weeks later a potential buyer of ours visited the home and promptly fell in love. They asked if the architect would meet with them, and they all showed up 3 days later.

They walked together inside and out, the buyer asking if dining room access to the terrace could be accomplished with French doors—and then came my revenge reward. The lady said, "I will need to have access from the maid's room to my children's bedrooms on the second floor. I presume that will be easy to do, and I am surprised it was not in your plans. I hope there is no structural reason preventing this access because I couldn't buy this house without that change."

I had to turn around for fear of laughing. However, before I did, I saw his facc...flushed, furious, embarrassed, deflated, you name it—but he did do it, and we sold the home to those people. Their young children are now out of college and the couple still live there—with a door from the maid's room connecting to the second floor bedroom area! It still makes me smile.

MERRILL LYNCH MISHAP...ALMOST

In the 70's, I was working in a boutique real estate agency which was sold to Merrill Lynch around 1982. I was considered their top broker—and indeed was number one in the country in the mid 80's. My reward was a trip to San Francisco with my husband on the corporate plane with the CEO. Such fun and excitement.

We had three days at *The Top of the Mark* hotel, leading up to the dinner and big award night. When my name was called to receive the number one trophy, I proudly made my way to the podium. The friendly CEO shook my hand and then reached for the handsome Bull statuary which was logo and brand of the company. He handed it over to me, and I gasped. It was large—and it was so heavy. I was caught off guard at the weight—and almost dropped it on the CEO's feet. I don't know to this day how I managed to stop that catastrophe—and walk back to my table with it! So I was number one alright, but I was also number one in the disaster category as well! It was a never-to-be-forgotten event.

Be Prepared: *Know Your Inventory*

―――――◆―――――

A Teaching Story

My husband used to ask me why I was going to work when I didn't have a customer or a client. My answer was the same then as it would be today.

The most important asset for a buyer or seller is a knowledgeable broker who knows every aspect of the marketplace. That means knowing every price range and nearly every property on the current market…a daunting task in any community. Buyers can suddenly become customers from a phone call, and an agent must be ready to discuss any and all price ranges suitable to the buyer immediately and without hesitation. Confidence and trust is built within those few minutes, and a buyer is impressed enough to let you become that buyer's agent. You must know your inventory in all price ranges so you can discuss the marketplace intelligently.

Case in point: After being in the business quite a while, I had the reputation of being a high-end broker. One day, I had a phone call from a young couple who were friendly with the son of clients of mine. They reached out for help even though they were assured I probably wouldn't know the houses in their low price range. When I could fully discuss their needs and talk about specific homes right there and then, they were amazed and wanted to work only with me. Indeed, one of the houses I discussed with them on that phone conversation was the property they bought upon seeing it the following weekend! Knowing your inventory and being able to describe it accurately instills confidence immediately. You have to know your inventory in all price ranges so that you are prepared to work with anyone asking for your services.

First Sale - 1970

T wo weeks after I received my broker's license, I was given 2 listings. Both of them were from Girl Scout families of the children I had in my troop. Of course, I advertised them under my name and received a call from a potential out-of-town buyer. He was an accountant and, although he did not buy the house he had called about, he did become my customer. In those days, not being allowed to belong to the MLS listing system unless I belonged to an office made it difficult to find properties in other ways. However, I did notice a FSBO ad in the local paper and drove to see it from the outside…and knew immediately this was the home my accountant would buy! I called the owner, an attorney, and asked if he would allow me to show and sell his house to my customer.

He agreed, gave me a one-day listing, and my first house sale was underway. Since I didn't belong to an agency, I had to negotiate a written binder to be signed by both parties—not an easy task between an attorney and an accountant! I bought a few binders at the Stamford Board of Realtors, took out my *"Principles and Practices of Real Estate"* bible and taught myself how to create a legitimate binder between a seller and a buyer.

In those days, there was no email, no fax, and no scanning, so I drove to the seller's lawyer's office and handed him the binder and 1% check. I was so nervous that the binder wasn't correct that I was shaking. The nice attorney finally looked up from scanning through the binder and said, "Your first sale?" I said "yes" and he said, "It won't be your last for sure. You are going to be an excellent broker. It's a perfect binder."

I was so relieved and that lawyer became a good friend throughout the years. The sale went through without a hitch, and neither buyer nor seller ever knew it was my first one!

PART II: LEARNING = EARNING...

INVEST YOUR TIME WISELY
(BE ALERT, SEE CHALLENGES AS OPPORTUNITIES)

How New Agents Can Compete with Established Agents

A Teaching Story

Residential real estate is a complicated, responsible business. A Realtor needs lots of education to become an agent/broker with expertise. Learning by joining an agency and paying attention to detail is a good way to get started. However, if you want to attain expertise quicker, you need to outwork every beginner; you need to document everything you learn every day; and you need to observe and process what the top brokers are doing to be knowledgeable. You need to spend time getting to know your area marketplace by attending every open house and by discussing the pros and cons with your peers. You need to be very alert to the condition of the property...if it needs lots of work, little work or no work. You will need to figure out if the inside of the house matches the outside, and note if there are any real drawbacks to the buyer. In other words, find a part of your real estate work that you can identify with and really become an expert in a relatively short time by reading, talking to established brokers, and doing hands-on training.

In this way you can become an expert in some phase of the business. This benefits both you and your customers/clients, as expertise and knowledge build trust. You will earn the respect of your manager and the other agents—and will undoubtedly attract customers/clients along the way. Everyone loves an expert!

Live-Work Space Challenge

Many years ago, I was referred to a darling young couple with little ones, who dreamed of having a chiropractic practice in our city. What was the problem? They did not have enough money for a conventional medical office space.

Being able to solve this challenge is one of the wonderful benefits of being a creative real estate agent. To be able to come up with a solution is so rewarding. There was a new type of residential development closer to downtown - and certain businesses were allowed to be part of the family home. They were called "raised ranches," where the one floor ranch-style plan was positioned directly over the other. Definitely not a Colonial...walking in the front door, there was a set of stairs going down to what could be play areas, office, etc., and stairs going up to family living.

It was a price they could afford, and allowable professional business could be conducted. It was perfect for their needs! They bought it, keeping their family on the upstairs level and giving him the space he needed on the lower level for his practice.

He worked there for several years making and saving money until he was able to purchase a beautiful, large property which would lend itself to a much more expansive, separate, medical space. He has made quite a name for himself and is still in that perfect home, enjoying the benefits of his success story. Nice people truly do deserve nice rewards.

LISTEN TO THE CHILDREN

I had two brand new listings on the market at the same time. I also had two great customers ready to buy! Both homes were special contemporaries, one without waterfront in the country, far away from the other property with its river setting, closer to downtown. I showed both houses to both customers—and wouldn't you know it—they both decided on the same country home!!

Now how to convince one of them to buy the river house? Then I would have both properties sold to both customers and neither would be disappointed and angry with me!

I said to the family with the young son…"Do you really want to be 20 minutes away from all the town activities for your son?" Danny, their son, answered for them, "I can fish in the river and get to the YMCA easily if I'm closer to town. The houses are almost the same," he continued. "Let's go see it again."

Well, we went back to the river property—and it was their son who sealed the deal. They really did like the house, and Danny's reasoning made a lot of sense. So, the unthinkable happened—Both great customers bought both great houses and lived happily ever after. In fact, one is still living there—and that was 30 years ago.

Lesson: Do pay attention to the children. Often they have more input than you think!

The 9th Broker

The seller was never happy—from beginning to end.

Perseverance and strength under duress pays off—gets the job done.

I have a favorite quote: "Sometimes it is better to be the first born, the second wife, and the third broker!"

Well in this case, the property stayed on the market for *9 years* …and I was chosen as the 9th broker. I did repeat the quote above to my seller, but there wasn't even a crack of a smile!

Even though it was a beautiful home, it was a very difficult transaction made so by the contentious seller who would not listen to this professional - and had probably never listened to anyone…

Almost at the end of our listing period, there came an offer of rental with an option to buy in two years. It was an unbelievable monthly rent from an upstanding CEO couple, and it was done.

Two years later, sure enough, the tenant wanted to exercise his option to buy—and after hard, long negotiations directly between the parties themselves (I stepped away from negotiating this one), a deal was struck.

We had been paid the two year rental fee, which the seller tried to get back—but this 9th broker finally did the impossible—collected the entire commissions and the 9 year house-on-the-market was really sold.

Once the Listing is Yours...

A Teaching Story

Let's have a discussion on how to keep your seller content—and perhaps even get his home sold!

Marketing is Number One...this is where understanding trends is so important. In today's world, online and social media are tantamount to getting the word out about your listing. Your office personnel can help you with that. Any property, medium price and above for your area, should have a brochure, flyer, or marketing piece in writing to go along with the actual listing sheet. It gives it an importance that the seller truly appreciates and elevates his opinion that you are thinking "out-of-the-box." Print advertising in newspapers and magazines has truly lost favor in this internet era, but sellers want to physically see their homes shown that way, so some print must be included.

Besides, sellers are always eager to see how their home compares to others—and so other sellers are looking at your ad, along with their own. And if yours stands out, who do you think will gain their confidence for that next possible listing? That type of advertising may not be so essential for buyers any more, but the sellers out there will definitely notice your individuality! Depending on the home, sometimes a video captures the essence of a lifestyle and tells a story about the house. Today, drones do a wonderful job outside and is a service offered by your photographer as part of his fee. Incidentally, an excellent photographer is always such an important factor in showing the personality of a home. Once you find a good one, stick with him/her. They are so vital to your success.

Sellers (and buyers) love attention. The more you show them you really care, the more they feel comfortable with you—and the "trust factor" is gained. You should be genuinely attentive until that property closes, and the sellers are relieved of their transaction responsibility.

If you have sold them another home, great! If they have moved away, do not lose touch. If you were entrusted to market their home, then they are important enough to remember forever. Hopefully, they will feel that way about you!

Looky-Loos Can be Buyers

I was lucky enough to be the listing broker on one of the most outstanding homes in all of Connecticut. I was so excited!

Because of its size and uniqueness, it took one and a half hours to show properly. There were many showings, not only to potential buyers, but to curiosity seekers who just wanted to view the interior. I was kept busy!

Then I received a call from a young man I knew who had gone to school with my daughter. He now lived in California, but had heard this home was on the market. It just happened to be in the same neighborhood as his family's house. He said, "I'm coming back East and would love to see it—I used to sneak in a midnight swim in that pool once in a while. I always wanted to see the inside."

Knowing the amount of time it took to show the home, and knowing that he was just curious to see the inside, I told him I would be happy to show him the property before or after another customer showing. He became noticeably irritated and said he wanted to see it as soon as he returned home and not wait on the sidelines for another person to view it. I agreed to take him when he wanted to go. But I was annoyed because he was just curious to see the inside!

Well, he did come back in a few days and he did see every-thing...inside and out. The unthinkable happened...he made an offer and actually bought this incredible property! I couldn't believe it, but I learned a valuable lesson: Never be so sure you can know someone else's motive in life, because you can't!

Follow Your Instincts

Years ago, I sold a lovely older home on a pond to a couple—and they enjoyed many years living there. Then one day everything changed. One of them was murdered by an intruder. It was so, so very sad, and the remaining spouse felt she had to leave her home and settle elsewhere. She gave me the listing.

We have rules, regulations and laws in real estate. One of the stipulations is that you are not obligated to provide psychologically impacted information, nor are you supposed to point out that type of stigma to the sale. It is an odd rule, but is probably in effect to guarantee the sale of the property.

As listing broker responsible to my seller, I found myself conflicted. As fate would have it, the potential buyer who was very interested in the home was a buyer of mine! They did make a good offer and it was accepted. Now I was really confused.

I called several real estate gurus and attorneys—and they all advised, "say nothing." It was a two-month closing and I felt more uncomfortable every day in not disclosing the murder. Everyone advised me against disclosure, and I really suffered. Finally three weeks before closing, I simply felt obligated to tell my buyers. I was so distraught for the seller and the buyer, but I felt it was the most honest solution, regardless of the outcome.

Imagine my astonishment when the buyers thanked me for sharing—but knew all about the tragedy from the day they first saw the house. I was so relieved to know the buyers were happy that I went against policy and informed them. They are loving their home to this day.

REAL ESTATE ETIQUETTE

A Teaching Story

Maybe this is a teaching page, but I am writing it as a story, also. When you become immersed in real estate for a number of years, you will acquire many outstanding and famous people as your customers and clients: It is natural as your name becomes known that this type of person will find you.

One of the most difficult restraints is not using your celebrity customer to gain more fame. It is hard not to drop a name which would certainly gain you another well-known person's interest. But that would be a No No in a broker's integrity. Famous people, for the most part, want anonymity and must trust you fully in that department.

Ideally, if you do a good job, they will recommend you to their celebrity friends without one word from you. That is the best way of having yourself promoted to top status. As a matter of fact, discretion and non-gossip are good and relevant attributes for all your customers/clients, regardless of their notoriety. The reason for selling or buying is very personal—and as an agent, you are bound to secrecy.

Case in point: A well-known business man with a thriving company was thinking of buying a home in the far North and asked me to find him a Realtor in that area…everything completely confidential because he wasn't quite ready to move permanently and didn't want his business to suffer prematurely. Complete trust is needed in a scenario of that type—and the broker has accomplished a great feat if that degree of the customer's confidence has been gained. "Mum's the word" is a really good saying in daily real estate life!

When the Buyer Chooses You

A Teaching Story

If a buyer is referred to you from a friend or someone you have worked for, that buyer usually wants to use you with no questions asked. They already have a good opinion of your real estate expertise. However, if a buyer calls on an ad, then you have to convince them that you are the best agent they can use.

Personality and warmth are always better displayed in person, but trust and respect can be garnered by how well you know your marketplace and how well you can present yourself in that cold call. It does take practice and self-confidence, but knowledge quickly aligns all the salesmanship talents. When you know what you are talking about, it's really easy and fun. Also, remember that real estate agents/brokers are usually thought of as "talkers." Actually, it is much more important to be a "listener." You would be surprised at how much is learned by just listening. Of course, you have to ask some pertinent questions, but many times one can zero in on the right home in just a few showings.

Paying attention to the buyers' wishes alerts you to the quickest and best way to a sale. Patience is another great virtue, as is not "rushing" a showing. It is ultra-important that the buyer feels you are trying to find the perfect house for his family, no matter how many houses need to be shown. Again, with practice and paying attention, you can erase a great number of showings by listening and zeroing in.

Buyers can be fickle...and need to be impressed by marketplace knowledge. They want to feel confident that you will find them the "perfect" property because you know and understand what they are looking for. The more they experience your expertise, the more they trust you to find their home.

Today, a buyer must sign a Buyer/Broker agreement contract, so the possibility of seeing multiple houses with multiple agents is significantly reduced. However, it still happens and many times that agreement is for a one-day showing and not 3 or 6 months. It is difficult for any buyer to sign a prolonged contract the first day he meets a strange agent through an ad! A few years back we had no written Buyer/Broker agreement, so the buyer had a chance to view houses with many agents and decide for him/herself if they felt comfortable. Times have changed radically—and "disclosure" is the word of today. It makes for lots of paperwork, but ultimately is for the benefit of everyone in this business.

Friends Forever

Forty years ago, I sold a fun home to a delightful young family. It was a contemporary with a swimming pool in a young neighborhood of similar homes. They seemed to enjoy the house for some years—and suddenly I received the phone call to list and sell. Unfortunately, they were divorcing, so I found a condo for the wife and another house for the husband and the children.

Some years later, he purchased a lovely lot next to the Long Island Sound and built a stunning home where he remained for many years. His grown daughter needed a home in our special waterfront community—and we found one for her and her family. After some joyful years, she decided to move on. We sold her house. Her father sold his oversized home and moved to a waterfront luxury condo that we sold him. He lived there many happy years with his lovely lady and then decided to move to a warmer climate, so we were called upon again.

I was the listing broker and an out-of-town broker had the buyer and also had her own condo she wanted to sell to her customer. The buyer finally called me out of desperation telling me he wanted to make an offer on my listing and his broker refused, still trying to sell him the condo that she owned—quite a predicament!

We worked it out, and he was able to buy our listing! My sellers moved happily to a warmer climate. I am still in touch with these wonderful people who will be my friends forever.

Late Sunday Strangers in the Night

One Sunday as I was leaving my office late, a young couple in a station wagon showed up as I was getting in my car. I asked if I could help direct them somewhere, and they said they needed a rental and a place to stay overnight. The car was filled to the brim with boxes and clothing. They looked as if they were permanently relocating.

Of course I reopened the office and invited them in. They looked exhausted and worried. I called my husband to tell him I would be another hour or so and then made a pot of tea to relax them. When I realized their rental budget could not get them any rental in my town, I called two of my broker friends in the less expensive areas contiguous to ours where they could be accommodated. One of these good brokers knew of a few rentals and a bed and breakfast inn for overnight.

Now don't forget this was about 8pm on a Sunday night. As the caring broker she was, she even arranged to meet them at the parkway exit so they wouldn't get lost on the way to the inn. She did rent them a condo the next day, and I knew they were in good hands. I never talked to the couple again.

About five years later, a handsome young man walked into my office, asking for me. I sat in the conference room with him and he explained he was building houses in my town. You guessed it! This young man was the gentleman who drove into my parking lot after a full day on the road from the South. He said he would like me to list and sell his houses because he never forgot my kindness and help when he and his lovely wife were running out of steam that Sunday night five years earlier.

I became his listing broker on many houses and subdivisions. The loyalty demonstrated by the gentleman in this story is heartwarming and inspirational. If you can be a sincerely caring person, the rewards are so much more than "money." They can be lifetime memories of the good within people.

SAME FAMILY, MULTIPLE HOUSES

The people I have met and worked with in this incredible real estate field are my heroes. They have all been so kind and caring towards me. My most favorite connection is when the whole family uses me as their broker. It has happened so often to lucky me—and I love the challenge.

I have been fortunate enough to have at least 75 people use me as their agent for the entire family. Sometimes brothers and sisters, sometimes spouses, even during divorces, sometimes the children and a few times even the grandchildren. Hundreds have used me over and over as they purchased other homes. Two or three listings for one party is normal, but 10 is outstanding, and I have done that as well. I remember once telling one of my favorite customers, "This is your final house. Do not call me again…You are here for good!" Four years later, I got the call and sold them one more home. I think they are there for the duration. But all bets are off!

To work for an entire family over the years is an exciting and exhilarating experience. The level of trust is beyond all words—and the satisfaction of knowing what is being expected of you is so rewarding. Some of these loyal, loving family members have amounted to 8 and 10 transactions in one family! That is an accomplishment of great pride. To be revered by family members who entrust their loved ones to you again and again is an honor in our business.

These are your friends for life—whether they move away or stay, you will never forget them or their kindness and respect. That sentiment alone gives you a lift as no other. I love this business!

A Gift From the Heart

One summer many years ago, I listed and sold a lovely lake property for my client who was moving to Florida. She needed a six-month closing and her buyers obliged and set the date for January 15th to accommodate her.

Along about December, this special lady called from her Florida home to tell me she was sending the keys and garage door openers in a shoebox and to please be careful not to lose them. The box arrived, and I put it unopened on a top shelf in our office.

A few days before our January closing, I opened the box to take those house items with me—and found another package wrapped in tissue. I carefully peeled back the tissue—and to my amazement found a huge Native American Squash Blossom turquoise necklace—truly a stunning old piece worth a great deal of money. I was shocked and called her immediately to tell her she must not have realized that this valuable jewelry was in that particular shoebox— and that she had added the other house necessities on top of it.

Well, this story ends with this wonderful client telling me that necklace was a surprise gift for me for selling her house so quickly and smoothly. Evidently her late husband had given the necklace

47

to her—and since it was not her style (but it was mine), she wanted me to own it. Such a lovely gesture, and I prize that gift from the heart to this day.

Surprises, The Unthinkable, and Quick Responses

A Teaching Story

When you love the real estate business as I do, the mornings don't come fast enough, so I can relish another incredible day at work.

That doesn't mean that there are not surprises, disappointment, scary events, etc. The day unfolds around excitement – meeting new people and challenging scenarios. Your desire to help people is overwhelming, and your days are filled with the energy to accomplish that.

However - and it is a BIG however - sometimes danger can be lurking and you must be aware and alert. Meeting strangers you've only met on the telephone at vacant homes, staying alone very late in your secluded office... these can be times when you need to be wary and smart. Never put yourself in a situation that could be compromising. Always think through situations and scenarios, and if anything appears "off" to you, trust your instincts!

A Couple of Conviction

One sunny day, I received a phone call from a couple asking if they could come to my office to meet with me. We arranged a time for the next day—and the conversation that ensued was truly interesting.

They were a delightful couple who told me they had seen a listing of mine from the outside and asked their broker to show it to them. The broker seemed reluctant to have them see it, saying it needed a lot of work and had other problems. (She was trying to sell them one of her own listings.) They grew wary and annoyed and decided to give me a chance to explain the house as the listing agent and show it to them.

It had a stunning setting and was a well-known, beautiful property. I explained it did need work, but could be truly spectacular with little effort. They loved it instantly and bought it! Theirs was a total and complete renovation. They took time and effort to do it all—and indeed it became one of the most exquisite estates in our city.

They lived there happily for many years with their two children and favorite dog (mine, too!) who could do a high five as well as a human. Of course, when it was time to move South, I was their listing broker—and to this day, I can call them dear friends who I will never forget.

Five Year Wait

I was called to view a home for listing and was asked if I knew of any great waterfronts. They were planning to move from their country house to the water. Well, yes, I could show them a perfect property on the market (a house I had built in 1987).

An hour later we were in the home—and this lovely couple fell in love! They tried to buy it right then and there but were told by the listing broker that it had already sold! She didn't tell me before we came to see the house—she told me after we had planned to buy it.

My customers were truly devastated...and we searched our water community for five years, trying to find another house. Nothing we looked at worked for them. So, finally I decided to leave my card in that beloved home mailbox, telling the owner that if he ever wanted to sell, I had a ready, willing and able buyer.

Well, what do you think? That owner called me and said he was going to put the property on the market in four months or so and to bring my buyers any time. Of course, I did and my couple bought it immediately from the front entry. The seller was delightful; the buyers were ecstatic and this story had a very happy ending. That was 14 years ago—and guess what—they are now moving out of state and who do you think has their listing? ME! And it was sold in 2019!

Nerves, Nervous, Nervy

A couple coming to the United States from Europe were spending 3 years here with a Fortune 500 company. The husband was a company specialist here to share his expertise. In 1986, it was possible to make more profit on your sold home when you left than even the extra salary offered by your company to relocate here for a few years.

The gentleman came alone and said he would pick the home without his wife seeing it. She was "expecting" and would not be able to accompany him in his search. Well, that bit of information truly made me nervous. We did find a house, and he went to contract on it. Those were the days before cell phone cameras, so he took Kodak photos and sent them to his wife.

He flew back just once when the baby was born, and then they both came here to settle down for those 3 years.

I remember being beyond worried that his wife would not like the house—and that would create a big problem. I went with them two days before the actual closing. I was a nervous wreck for her reaction to the home…a sigh of relief—she loved it and they lived there

3 years and then gave me the listing to sell when they were return-ing to Europe. They did make 28% profit on its sale—and they were thrilled. A perfect ending for them and relief beyond words for me.

Handling Luxury Properties

A Teaching Story

Of course, everyone would like to be a luxury, high-end real estate agent! It does take extra time and effort, but any ambitious broker can accomplish that.

Remember, the only difference between you and that wealthy customer or client is the number of zeros at the end of their financial statements. That should make you feel less intimidated. As a rule, they are all very connected...by business, by lifestyle, by similar interests, such as art, theatre, charities, sports, and travel.

Since all these avenues are prone to finding high net-worth individuals, make an effort to get involved with your local art groups, museums, and theatre, so you will have opportunities to associate with the people you would like to do business with.

I became a luxury broker by the "Time Method." After selling so many homes in a growing area, my $200,000 house became $500,000 in 10 years and $1,000,000 in 20. So celebrating a 50-year career now puts me in the true high-end category. Because houses are not going up in price as they did in those days, things will not be as easy for new agents today.

Luxury real estate is not the end-all either. Good bread and butter lower-priced properties are always welcome. The main lesson here is to become comfortable with all income levels, so that when you have the opportunity to acquire a listing or a buyer, value doesn't matter. Getting the house sold or finding a home for the buyer should be your only consideration.

Seller/Buyer — Same Broker

Faith, respect and trust are always essential in the real estate business, but when dealing with your seller AND your buyer, it is tantamount to succeed in satisfying both parties.

Years ago, we didn't have buyer agents and seller agents. One was very often the listing broker selling her own listing to her own buyer. It was always one of the more difficult transactions, but you did it!

Today, buyers' and sellers' brokers are totally separate. Years ago, I had a very special estate property with large acreage on the market. It belonged to two families; one living on one side of the property and the other home completely on the other side of the property. Once on the market, there was immediate interest from several local customers…one in particular.

After showing him the houses and land, instinct told me he would be the ultimate buyer. He was enthralled with the property and truly understood its quality. My sellers asked me about all the potential buyers who had seen it—and I said I had just shown it to *the one* who would actually buy it. I just knew it…without yet having an offer in hand and having just met that potential buyer for the first time. There was never a question with my sellers that he was **MY** customer/buyer, and he must have felt the same way, because he never questioned my integrity and seemed to have complete confidence in me.

Well, we did put it together—and he and his lovely wife have lived there for years, relishing every moment. I so appreciated his honest, forthright approach to that sale. I admire both of them more than I can say and count them as dear friends—not just customers/clients. Now for the clincher…they still send me a gift every holiday time. I think it is supposed to work the other way around. Bless their hearts!

Estate Listing

The phone rang at Juner Properties in the 1990's, and I answered. "I would like to speak to June Rosenthal," the voice said. I introduced myself and the gentleman told me he was in Switzerland, but owned a 36-acre house in Stamford and he would like me to get a presentation ready for his return in a few weeks. His landscape lady would let me into the house and would show me the whole estate. (She is my dear friend to this day.)

I visited that incredible property at least four times, writing up my presentation with great care. Many photos and pages later, I was ready!

The gentleman called me the next day from Gstaad, Switzerland and said, "I will be home in a week. I wanted you to know that you will have the listing on my home. And I don't need to see your presentation." I was truly startled—and of course, excited—but I couldn't understand why he made that decision without meeting me and checking out my evaluation.

The story evolved when we met a week later. He told me that when he was getting ready for bed in a hotel, he had noticed a magazine on his pillow. It was called *Estates* (which showcased leading estates of the world) and right there, a few pages in, was my photo and a lovely bio. He said he made a decision immediately that I was his broker...no matter what! I listed the estate—and guess what—I also sold it myself. A true and fabulous real estate story.

Educated Opinion (Being Sure of Yourself)

Years ago, I was asked to make a sales presentation on listing a huge estate of 75 acres owned by several CEOs of a major cosmetic company. The meeting was in their NYC office with principals and attorneys present. We met in a gigantic conference room with an enormous table—and I was excited and nervous—but had done my homework and was very well prepared. It lasted about two hours, and I had given them a selling price of $9-9.2M and an asking price of $9.4M. They argued that they would NEVER get that price, but when it was on the market less than a month, a buyer offered $9M, and my sellers were dumbfounded. They shouted "We'll take it!" I said, "No, we will meet them in the middle at $9.2M."

"No, no," they said, "We'll lose them."

Well, the buyer gladly paid $9.2M and the sellers were astounded. There is a lesson here on how to be a hero. Being prepared and having facts to bear out your pricing (high or low) is vital. It leads to trust, because you have studied the market and are willing to give your educated opinion–so stick to it! That really impresses sellers and buyers alike.

One-in-a-Million

A late Sunday morning call came in on my $3M water-front listing. He sounded sincere and wanted to see the property that same afternoon. I told him I would see if the owner would be able to accommodate such short notice. Being the cooperative seller that she was, she said yes. I made the date for 3pm. There was no "Google" in those days, and it was Sunday with no way to check his credentials. We both took a chance, clearly on instinct alone.

He showed up pretty much on time in a convertible, was very friendly, and took well over an hour looking closely at every detail inside and out. The owner was in her office the whole time per my instructions and the potential customer greeted her in his informal, pleasant manner when viewing the office. He did over-compliment the house and furniture—and she was thinking he was showing great interest. He left, and I ran in to tell the owner that she shouldn't get excited over the showing as things in her price range never happen fast and that he seemed to be a bit of a character!

Five minutes later, the doorbell rang and I opened the door. There he stood, and said he had forgotten something. He had forgotten to make an offer on the property—and how much was it? I was pretty much speechless, but asked him to come in to discuss things further. I was thinking that he was really crazy, so I had to be careful. When I told him $3M, he casually said okay, and also wanted to know if the furniture was for sale, because he didn't have enough for such a big house.

It was time to engage the owner in this unbelievable conversation—and I was still extremely wary of the whole outcome. Well, here's the conclusion in a nutshell. He did buy the home for $3M, and most of the furniture—and on Monday, I found out he was the CEO of a large, very well-known company, and everyone lived happily ever after...

I am still in touch with that seller and with the buyer too after almost 30 years... and I love them both. Real Estate allows friendships to flourish like no other business... forever, many times!

PART III: Refining Your Work and Expecting the Unexpected

Communication...the Secret Ingredient

A Teaching Story

Of all the miraculous attributes we were given in our short lifespan was the ability to communicate by voice, by body language, by actions, and by writing. Particularly in the real estate field, communication is vital. Keeping in touch with your buyers/clients is foremost and essential.

Remember, you are undoubtedly competing with many agents in your area, so you must do something different to set yourself apart from the others. Being available for your contacts is one way to garner attention and stand out from the crowd. The buyer should be informed about every new listing which fits his criteria—and the seller needs special information about competitive listings on the market. The more you inform, the more likely the customer and the client/seller will be loyal to you. Penning a note or sending a card is always welcome. It simply shows that you are thinking of them. If you want to keep a listing until it is sold (as opposed to having another agent take over when the listing contract is up), then show the seller you care by paying them close attention.

Planned and intentional communication is tantamount to being remembered! If your potential buyer starts wandering off with other brokers, then more attention is needed.

It is really easy to find unique ways of keeping in touch. Use your ingenuity...with email, texting, emojis, phone calls, notes, simple newsletters and cards. Find your very own creative way to keep your name in their minds.

It actually keeps you "thinking" and on your toes which is good in your business and personal life! Communication...the secret ingredient for success, respect, and reputation.

BUYER AND SELLER CHEMISTRY

Forty years ago, I had a call from a referred customer asking me about a historic Colonial she had seen from the outside and was intrigued enough to want more information about it. The house had never been on the market in my real estate career, but I told her I would check it out. It was a beautiful, stately older home in a coveted area and owned by an elderly lady who had lived there for years. I tried everything to contact her, but couldn't.

Finally, in my frustration, I left a note in her mailbox and said that I had a customer interested in her home and would she please call me. Well, a few days later, she called...a lovely lady who had lived there with her husband for over 50 years! She asked me to stop by so she could meet me—and I did. She was so charming, and we had a lovely tea time together. She then asked me to bring my customer so she could meet her also.

A few days later, my customer (who was a stranger to me) and I paid the owner a visit. They liked each other instantly and had a good time learning about one another. They both had enjoyed a 7-children family—and had many travels in common...a cemented relationship if ever there was one!

Yes, that special house was sold to my exceptional customer, and a lifetime of happiness was born again in that precious old home. And that is the magic of real estate. For the most part, it is happiness forever! It is a perpetual cycle of regenerating joy.

First Investment, Trusting in People

My first year on my own in real estate was difficult. Acquiring listings was almost impossible because I was not allowed on MLS without belonging to an office. All sellers wanted to have the exposure which the Multiple Listing Service offered them.

About six months into the real estate business, I received a phone call from a couple wanting to sell their home. They had seen one of my many ads in the local paper asking sellers to call me. I visited them the next day and found them to be an elderly man and wife seeking to move to a warmer climate after 40 years of Connecticut weather! Their house was adorable—and they had a darling 1 bedroom guest cottage—both houses on 2-3/4 acres in a 1 acre zoned area, which made it a true gem.

I envisioned my first investment property with 2 houses to rent. (That would take care of a mortgage payment and all other property expenses.) But they would have to trust me regarding the price of their home, and if indeed they would feel any reservations dealing with me, both as a listing broker and then buying it for myself. I really was conflicted, but I decided to approach them honestly and find out their feelings.

Well, they were delighted to sell to me and said they trusted me completely. I had suggested a listing price of $125,000 with a selling price of $124,000 (+or-). So, I paid the asking price and took no commission—and they were overjoyed. It was a very special property which I kept rented for many years. I finally subdivided the little guest house on its own acre. Both houses were sold about 12 years later—the little house sold to its renters who eventually built an incredible home with the cottage as its base. It is most unique and they live in it to this day and love it more each passing year. I also sold two houses in later years to the tenants in the main house. Moral: My first investment might have been the best of many in my life.

Instant Rapport

Many, many years ago, I had a phone call from a German customer on an ad I had placed. The caller was eager to see a Tudor home near our water community. Of course I said "yes" and met him at the house.

I liked him immediately... such a warm personality. He was planning to spend a few years in the USA to expand his business. He liked the house, but decided he wanted more of a country home on several acres. However, he loved the Tudor style.

Through a referral, I was talking to another seller with a Tudor and tennis court on several country acres. The seller was most difficult with everything—and we had not come to a "meeting of the minds" on anything, including price.

It was one of my most difficult sales ever, but after a week of deliberation and the buyer's exemplary patience, we finally put the transaction together. My delightful buyer lived there with his charming wife for quite a few years enjoying every moment and inviting my husband and me to lovely parties.

Instant rapport doesn't happen often, but it needs to be recognized if it happens. He and his wife have been back in Germany for quite a while, but we have never lost touch. He even met us and chauffeured us around when we took a vacation cruise on the Rhine River and docked in his city.

The real estate business truly opens up a world of fine people—and friends forever. Learn to trust your instincts!

PERSEVERANCE (...ON ONE CONDITION)

When I was a broker of only a few years, I was fortunate enough to get a call on my ad from the CEO of a Fortune-500 company. They were relocating from Florida to my Connecticut home town and were in the process of building their offices. He sounded so pleasant, and I was so excited. He made a date to see houses within two weeks. Well, I spent hours seeing many homes with the criteria he needed—and was all ready for the big Monday. However, on Sunday I received a call from him telling me they had arrived and had taken a ride in their rental car and found the perfect new home on the border of the next town—and bought it directly from the builder! I was beyond disappointed. He was sincerely apologetic and said he and his wife would like to take me to lunch on Monday instead of viewing houses. I thanked him for his offer and said I would love to meet them for lunch, on one condition...that they would take a drive with me and at least see the outside of the three best homes I had picked out for them. They said "yes" and after lunch we took that drive.

I know you have already guessed the outcome. They loved all 3 properties and bought the lakefront after canceling the purchase of the builder's new house. They were super special people—AND from that one sale, I made 24 more sales within 16 months to his associates who were also moving to their new headquarters. That's not all—when they all relocated again 7 to 10 years later, I listed every one of those houses and got them sold! Not only that, I still hear from many of those great people at holiday time. I owe it all to a fine gentleman who wanted to show kindness to a disappointed broker. He was truly responsible for my ultimate success in this business.

A Windfall: The Benefits of Maintaining a Friendship

Forty-five years ago, a young builder walked into my real estate office at the time—and asked for me by name. I greeted him, and we sat down to discuss his needs. He was in the process of interviewing agents for his project. He had purchased a large tract of land and was going to develop it into one-acre lots with 40 contemporary type houses. That was a huge subdivision in those days (as it would be today) and I was being asked to work with him and list these homes as they were built! It was an extraordinary and exhilarating prospect for any broker!

Well, I did get those listings, and the builder and I built a solid relationship.

Years later, he acquired another beautiful tract of land and gave me those 30 houses to list as well. I also sold him an estate of 21+ acres and again listed those homes and sold them. The point is, he was my friend, and I was his Realtor...forever. He is retired now, but he receives a holiday card and little gift from me every year, and he and his delightful wife are friends to this day! Imagine what one meeting can accomplish when two people respect and trust each other. Amazing!

One Couple—10 Sales!

Forty years ago, I sold a house to a delightful young couple with two very young children. They were both so dear and appreciative, and the wife was always recommending me, and I sold several homes to her friends. Four or five years later, this beautiful young lady passed away.

Around the corner there lived a lovely divorced lady with two children, and in time, the widower and she became acquainted and that friendship grew into love and marriage.

They decided to start their life together by selling his house and her house and purchasing their very own home. That was the beginning of many buying and selling years—ten transactions in all with one couple! And these awesome people are dear friends to this day. They always remember me at holiday time and my birthday—and I dearly love them both.

The most wonderful and rewarding part of the residential real estate business is the people you meet and keep in your heart forever. They are so special to me.

Sign Benefits

One Saturday, a message was left on my phone that came from someone who'd seen my sign on a new house in our water community. Could I show it to them on Sunday? A good agent is *always* ready and able to accommodate a real estate request—and I was always prepared.

It was a really great showing with immediate interest on this buyer's part. So what question do you think they asked me right there and then? "Do you think we're crazy to buy such a large home for just the two of us?" Of course, you know what my internal instinct would be on a multi-million dollar property which was both my listing—and would be my sale if they bought it! However, I needed to bypass the excited thoughts about the healthy commission and answer with my heart and mind...so I said, "Yes, I do think you are crazy—BUT if you love it and can afford it—that must be left entirely up to you both." So they bought their dream home—and I became the listing broker on their previous home – which I also sold myself! I love this precious couple who have referred me to many others, including their son. Honesty always prevails.

Speaking Up Led to Mutual Respect

A well-known sassy attorney was referred to me. Just talking to him on the phone alerted me to his caustic ego and disrespect for brokers in general! We met the following weekend, and he was accompanied by his lovely wife. He sat in the front passenger seat immediately (usually a sign of the decision maker) and didn't hold the door for his wife. He said he didn't have time to waste, and he hoped I wasn't showing him "garbage." I decided enough was enough, and I pulled over to the side of the road. I turned to face him—and these are the words that came out of my mouth. "I wouldn't think of wasting your valuable time—so I have three properties to show you. Do you want to see the home you are going to buy first, second or last?" I said it with a straight, non-smiling face—and his body language told me I had made my point. He said, "Well, let's see it first since you are so sure of yourself."

We saw it ten minutes later. He declined to view the other two—and bought the first one. He was quite subdued during the weeks leading to the closing…and he actually became a friend and sent me several referrals.

Moral: Being able to "read" your customers (and clients) is a priceless talent. Listening is more important than talking, but there are definitely times when speaking up is imperative. It shows that you work best when there is mutual respect and knowledge. I have never seen it fail...not once!

Intruder

A Teaching Story

Because it was quiet and conducive to mapping out the next day's plans, I often sat in my office working until 7pm, long after everyone else managed to "call it a day." One such spring evening, I was on my next day's schedule when a man walked in the door that I was facing. I did not like his looks and immediately felt fear. He walked back to my glass windowed office and stood in the doorway. I didn't get flustered and asked how I could help him.

He said he wanted to see a few houses and could I take him out right now! I told him it was 7pm and no one wants their home shown at dinner time. I had an alarm button on the wall within arm's reach—and was ready to punch it. I told him this with my hand over it—and he literally ran out the office door. I got up and locked the door but noticed his car was parked way up the street and not right in front of our free-standing little building. I did call the police, but never heard anything more.

My office was at an intersection of three main roads, but I always felt safe. After that incident, I kept that front door locked! Realtors really have to be cautious and never show empty houses to call-ins or strangers. Always take another person with you under those circumstances…and trust your instincts!

CALENDAR KISMET

A young couple decided Connecticut was not going to be the best area for commuting to work, so I sent them to my old hometown of Chappaqua, NY, which would be a very short distance to his new job. I picked the Realtor who sold them a home in November and they were delighted.

In December, I received a well-made marketing piece calendar from that selling broker, depicting Chappaqua's old historic days. I tucked it away in my home desk drawer until I would have time to browse through the months.

At the end of January, I came across the calendar while looking for something else in my drawer. Often, I worked late in my home office and this was one of those midnight catch-up times. I began to check out the historic photos one month at a time. I came to July and saw the annual parade festivities in downtown Chappaqua on July 4th.

I began to remember those fun summer days, recognizing store fronts and, in particular, Cadmans drug store where the school kids could sit at the counter and enjoy an ice cream cone or a fizz drink from a fizz maker.

There were photos of the parade, the fire engines, the red, white and blue banners and flags everywhere—and lots of people watching. Suddenly, my eyes caught a woman with a very large sun hat holding the hand of a 10 or 11 year old girl in saddle shoes. There came a burst of memory and the excitement of discovery. A magnifying glass confirmed it…it was my Mother and me! I was truly overwhelmed and astonished—60 years later—and to think I almost missed catching that incredible synchronicity!

So what is it that allows this type of good "karma" to show up for us at a particular time in our lives? So many things are a forever mystery—and this is definitely one of them.

World Connections-Mind Boggling

Scene One

Maybe 35 years ago I received a call to list a home for a lovely couple referred to me. It was a fine property, and I was delighted to be their listing broker. There was only one problem—their last name was so different and difficult, I had a hard time pronouncing it! We had the home for about 5 months from listing to closing—and I think it was only in the last month that I was able to say their last name correctly. We actually made a joke about it. They moved to Nashville.

Scene Two

My husband, Rolf, and I are in a Land Rover on our way to Tiger Tops in Nepal. That's where you ride elephants to find tigers to photograph. A gentleman joined us from another Rover headed away from the Lodge. He sat next to Rolf and explained he had left important papers back at the Lodge and had to retrieve them. Rolf and he found that they had mutual business friends in Nashville— and I piped up and said, "I only know one person who moved there about 15 years ago," and I pronounced the name correctly after all my months of practice. Well this man almost fell out of the Rover. He said that was his accountant and dear friend!

Not only that, but the briefcase he was going back to retrieve had important papers for my former client, his friend! The whole thing was mind-boggling! It was just happenstance that he got into our vehicle and started talking. I am sure this type of coincidence can happen in any business, but the real estate world is always "on the move," so maybe there is more chance of it happening.

SMALL WORLD

One morning, I received a phone call from out-of-town customers who wanted to see a house I was advertising in the *New York Times*. They were now living in the south and wanted to move back east.

It was a rainy, muddy spring day, and the home they called on was ¾-finished new construction. The driveway to the garage was a running mud river! We finally made it because my Land Rover was the perfect car for that miserable weather. I showed the house, and they loved it. The builder was working there, and they were impressed with him. We left about 3:30 in the afternoon with the rain really coming down. As I was beginning to back up, the builder appeared and asked if he could ride on my running board so he could reach his car on the street without tramping through the mud. Of course, I said yes, and he jumped on.

I rolled down my window so he would have a better grip and proceeded to back out. The builder asked me to give his best to Rolf, my husband, and my new buyer suddenly exclaimed, "Rolf? Your name is Rosenthal? Rolf Rosenthal? Is that your husband?" The outcome of the conversation was that this complete stranger worked with Rolf twenty years before in New York City and had lost contact. This was happening in Connecticut—nothing to do with New York, so he was understandably in shock.

They did buy that home, and Rolf and he renewed their friendship for the 12 years they remained in their home. Sadly, he died and his lovely wife moved to be with her family in California. We probably would have never known anything if the builder hadn't asked about Rolf. The real estate business is amazingly full of that kind of "small world" encounters.

April Showers

One lovely spring day, I was showing houses to a delightfully shy elder couple. I did most of the talking that day to put them at ease. We spent 3 or 4 hours visiting smaller properties that would be the right size for them.

Our last house on the list was in a beautiful community, and they seemed to be eager to see this particular home. In those days, there was no separate listing agent and buyer's agent. You were just "the broker" who called the seller and made an appointment to view the property.

Well, I did that, and we were right on time. I used the lockbox, opened the door and proceeded to show the house. When we went up the stairs, we thought we heard music, so I called out, "We're here…anyone home?" Hearing no answer, we proceeded. It was a three bedroom home and we entered the master.

I heard water running, so I said, "I think the owners must have left the radio and a faucet on." Stepping further into the room, we saw the master bath door open and two people having a jolly old time in the shower! My shy customers stood like stone statues and in complete shock. We hurried out of the room, and they didn't say a word all the way back to my office.

I did call the sellers and they were not at all embarrassed—they casually just said they thought I was coming the following day. Needless to say, my customers did not buy that home, but they did buy another—one that was thankfully vacant!

NOT ALWAYS HAPPILY EVER AFTER

A lovely young lady was referred to me, and we made a date to see houses with her fiancé over the weekend. They were getting married in 2 months. When we all started toward my car, he ran over to the passenger side and quickly jumped in saying, "I make all the decisions!" His girlfriend opened the rear door and got in herself.

At the end of the second house showing, the lady said, "I could really live in that last house. It was so open and airy and I love the views." He snapped back at her, "Since it is all my money, it will be all my decision, and I didn't like it. So forget it!"

I had heard enough! I pulled over to the side of the road and told him I was uncomfortable with his attitude and suggested he continue looking at homes with another broker. He was furious and wanted to continue that day with what I had planned to show them. He didn't utter another word until the last house and then said he would buy that one...he made the decision. She had nothing to say about it. It was truly alarming for a couple getting married! The property was purchased, and they were supposed to live happily ever after. She had a baby a year later, and they were divorced a year after that. Of course, I did not get that listing. She was very apologetic about it, but he never talked to me again after the closing.

I had thought many times of having a heart to heart with her, but there is a fine line between professionalism and personal interference. I just wish I could have saved her the heartbreak I absolutely knew she would endure. That was definitely one of my sadder sales.

Scary

Rather than leave it empty, sometimes we handled rentals for our clients when they left their home for an excessive time period. Such was the case some years back. The house owner was overseas for a few years and a tenant was chosen—not so much for the rental money—as it was to have the home occupied.

A young man was given that opportunity. Several months later, the owner called me and said the rent had not been paid since the first month! He asked if I would follow up. I called several times and could not reach the tenant. I decided to visit him in person and travelled to the house after 6pm when I thought he would be home from work.

He was home, was drunk and opened the door with a can of beer in his hand. He ushered me to the kitchen, and I asked if he had a money problem since he had not been paying rent. He was visibly agitated and reached over and grabbed a butcher's knife and brandished it in front of my nose. He got even more belligerent, and I was getting nervous. However, I was careful not to show my fear and spoke in a determined voice. I stood up and said, "You need to pay for your rental—and quickly—or you will have to be evicted. I need a check right now for the last three months, and if you are not able to make it out in your present condition, give me your checkbook, and I will do it for you."

He looked glassy-eyed and furious, but he got his checkbook from the side table and handed it to me. I stood the whole time making out the check and gave it to him for a signature. He never put that big knife down until he signed the check. I picked up that knife and put it in a kitchen side drawer. He saw me put it away, but remained seated. I took the check and went out the closest door in the kitchen. I walked hurriedly to my car. I made a decision never to go alone again in a confrontation like that one. I was lucky! He wound up having to be evicted six months later...

At Knife's Edge

Six months into real estate and two days on the job in a small real estate firm I had joined …this really happened. I was alone at my desk at 9 am preparing for a customer. The door opened and a distraught woman entered with a long knife! I asked if I could help and she screamed, "Where is she? I will kill her!"

I somehow managed to get her to the chair at the side of my desk and talked quietly to calm her down. "She is not taking my husband from me!" she began screaming again. I told her no one was there but me and being that upset would only make things worse. I quietly made a hot cup of tea, but the knife was still in her hands. I expected my customer at 10am and it was now 9:35. I needed to get her out of the office, into her car and gone before they arrived.

I told her she should confront her husband together with a marriage counselor and try to iron things out instead of brandishing a knife and perhaps doing harm to someone and ending up in jail for life—in which case she would have lost her husband anyway. She had calmed with the tea. And the knife was now lying on my desk. I slowly moved it to my side of the desk and told her the knife was definitely NOT the answer and would only harm her in the end. She watched me but didn't try to retrieve it.

She left as my customers drove in. They said they were expecting an exciting day, anticipating finding a great home. I told them that was the type of excitement I loved best!!

Money - Evil Corruption

Years ago, I met and sold an unusual hunting lodge / home to a young couple. They lived there for a long time. One day, they walked into my office and said they wanted to sell their home and move to an estate-like property. They also said they had driven everywhere in our city and felt there was no home big enough or handsome enough for their taste. They had decided to go to the wealthiest town close by and asked if I could show them houses there.

I knew of just one exquisite, older historic home that had just been completely and remarkably redone by fine builders—and I said, "come with me right now, and I will show you your dream home right here in your city." They jumped in my car and bought that house in an hour!

Many years passed, and then came a call to sell that property. They had bought a brand new state-of-the-art house, but, unfortunately, had not kept up their historic home. Houses can go downhill really fast if no attention is paid to upkeep. For the sales price they wanted and the recession upon us, we could not attract a buyer. Finally, we planned an auction, and sure enough, the auctioneer found a buyer! Many negotiations later—and excessive work by my real estate partner who acted as their unpaid manager, the deal was put together...only to find that the sellers had cheated us out of our earned $65,000. His attorney lied to both the auctioneer and to us. We got nothing. Our buyer was the only upstanding participant, and we didn't want him and his family to lose the property, so we let it go.

How incredibly sad when people sell their souls for money! That $65,000 will never bring them joy, as things always have a way of working out in the end.

Anyway, they will go down in my playbook as the only client in fifty years who cheated me out of a commission. Quite a good record, wouldn't you say? But I will remember this unethical couple forever.

A Sinking Feeling

Oh, yes—I will never forget THAT phone call late Sunday morning. I had sold a family Colonial to a lovely young couple on a neighborhood street near my office. I was home that Sunday and picked up the ringing phone. Hysteria greeted me on the other end exclaiming, "Oh, please come quick! My Weber grill is sinking and so is the children's jungle gym—and so is the whole back lawn. I am looking out my kitchen window and everything is disappearing!! My husband is away with the children, and I think I may be going crazy!" She was in a full-blown panic, as she screamed this message to me over the phone.

I told her I would drive right over, but to call 911 and alert the fire department. I jumped in my car and sped over there to find that she was 100% correct. The whole backyard had sunken at least 5 or 6 feet. It was an unbelievable sight. I told her to be grateful that her kids were away and that no one was injured. The city looked into it and found that their street, even though it was part of the big subdivision, had underground water problems on several of the lots—and no houses should have been permitted to be built on those lots.

Needless to say, this nice couple moved to another home—and I am friends with her to this day. That nightmare/daymare happened at least 35 years ago, but I will never forget the sheer terror in her voice. Today, we joke about it, but it was no joke then.

Again and Again

As one can imagine, there is a huge variety of homes in the residential sector. Of course, agents have favorites, but our job is to find *your* **happily** forever home, not ours! Many times, we sell a buyer a house that we really don't like, but it has to be the buyer's choice. However, when a broker loves a home, many times he/she will sell it more than once.

I built a house on the water meant to be a retirement residence for my husband and me ten years down the road. It was truly spectacular...not too large and with a beachfront setting. Perfect for us—until a buyer showed up even before it was finished and offered me so much money that I had to sell it.

Since that time in 1987, I have sold and listed that property four times. I loved that home, and it was always a joy to have people live there and love it as I did. There was another waterfront home not far from the one above... same thing—I loved that classic property also and managed to sell it four times.

But don't misunderstand—every home is a precious commodity to its owners. And every broker needs to understand that. The same effort and enthusiasm must be applied to EVERY property.

Your sole responsibility is to get the home sold for the seller. There can be no favoritism shown. No matter what your feelings are, you work diligently for your clients/customers.

Too Much Gossip!

This lovely spring day, I received a call from a waterfront owner who was interviewing agents eager to list his exquisite and expensive home. I arrived, and both he and his wife offered me coffee on the pool terrace overlooking the water and the New York City skyline. It was a truly breathtaking view—and I really wanted to list this property for sale.

The husband took me on the grand tour—and I was getting more and more intrigued. I told him I would be back in a few days with my full presentation, including the suggested asking and selling price. I did that, and they seemed to be impressed.

He told me he had three other agents giving him their price and strategies—and he would let me know. He called in about a week and asked me to meet with him again. I was really excited, as I liked him and his wife as much as I liked the property. He told me the listing was mine! And then, he asked if I wanted to know why he chose me? Of course, I said, "yes," and this was his answer.

He had told the other agents, as he had me, who he was interviewing. The others were large, national agencies and mine was small— only 14 agents. He said all their time was spent finding fault with my small boutique company, and he decided I must be really excellent to have every one of them disparaging my name. He also loved the word "boutique" for his home. He decided I must be the best broker to get all that adverse attention.

There's a lesson here: Don't discuss competitors. Do your own thing in an honest, personable way with plenty of pertinent facts about the marketplace and your very own marketing strategy. Finding fault with competitors does not put you in the best light.

So, There You Have It!

I do hope that the business of residential real estate has a much different "feel" after reading this book. Almost everyone has some connection to real estate.

Let this little book teach you BIG lessons in everyday life. In particular, learn to love the challenges of residential real estate and the people who comprise that world… Translate that love into action and euphoric financial success through ingenuity and drive. The result: *Houses for Love & Money* - the heart and wallet intertwined.